An Exciting and Adventurous View of History

Book One of the

*Saving History Series*

# Time

# Keeper

Robert Starnes

Novel Study by Patricia Carpenter

Copyright © 2018 by Starnes Books LLC.

All rights reserved. This book or any portion thereof may not be reproduced or used in any manner whatsoever without the express written permission of the publisher, Starnes Books LLC, except for the use of brief quotations in a book review.

Published by Starnes Books LLC
Created by Patricia Carpenter
Edited by Carpenter Editing Services, LLC

ISBN: 978-1-7325803-3-6 (sc)


First Printing, 2018

# Contents:

Book Summary

Main Characters

Chapter Summaries

Vocabulary

Questions and Answers

Themes

Activities

Tests and Answers

Worksheets

# Book Summary

Ian was given an antique watch for his seventeenth birthday from his parents. Through a series of dream memories, forgetting a year of his life, the loss of his best friend Kayla, and the help of a new friend, "Jax", Ian was about to experience the magic of the watch. Somehow, on what he thought to still be his seventeenth birthday, Ian returned home to his eighteenth birthday with no memory of what had happened during the past year, and even Jax couldn't help him. Ian needed to find out what happened to his best friend, who was changing time and history, and why they were doing it before it was too late and Kayla was gone forever. But finding Kayla could unpredictably change Ian's own history. What should he do?

# Main Characters

Ian: a typical high school boy

Ian's mom and dad

Kayla: Ian's best friend, who lives in the same apartment building

Jax: the man from Ian's "dreams" trying to help figure things out

Alexis: a woman from the future who gives Kayla a gift for Ian

History Series – Time Keeper

Novel Study by Patricia Carpenter

# Summaries: Prologue and Chapters 1-4

**Prologue:** Junior has been having very disturbing dreams. Through them, he has begun to realize that if he doesn't find out who is going back and changing history, and soon, he may no longer exist.

**Chapter 1:** At breakfast, Ian receives a special watch from his parents for his seventeenth birthday. After he dresses for the day, Ian finds his parents have left the apartment with no note, so he decides to go to one of their favorite places in the city to look for them. With no luck in locating them, he later returns home to his eighteenth birthday party, with no memory of the past year!

**Chapter 2:** Chapter 2 tells what happened to Ian during the year he was away at his new school, that he doesn't remember, and his return for his surprise 18th birthday party.

**Chapter 3:** Now that Ian is away at a new school without Kayla, she has to begin her senior year of high school without him. On her way to school, Kayla meets a woman, Alexis, which she had met before but has forgotten. Alexis asks Kayla to do her a favor, to give a special birthday present to Ian for her. Kayla agrees without knowing what the gift is.

**Chapter 4:** Ian wakes up in the taxi he thinks is taking him to Central Park to look for his parents. Instead he sees its night time and they are headed to his apartment in Brooklyn. When he gets out of the taxi and goes up to his apartment, he is surprised by guests there for his 18th birthday party. This is too much for him to take, so on the advice of his father; Ian goes to bed to get some much needed sleep.

Novel Study by Patricia Carpenter

## Vocabulary: Prologue and Chapters 1-4

Write these words on the board and have the students define each word, use in a sentence, find synonyms, locate in the novel, and discuss whole class or small group:

notion

anticipation

antique

aggressive

bizarre

negotiations

meager

devours

grasps

exhausted

Novel Study by Patricia Carpenter

Name:_____  Date:_____

## **Vocabulary** Quiz Prologue and Chapters 1-4

Directions: Choose the word that completes the sentence correctly. Write the letter of that word in the blank.

Word Bank:

| | |
|---|---|
| A. notion | F. anticipation |
| B. antique | G. aggressive |
| C. bizarre | H. negotiations |
| D. meager | I. devours |
| E. grasps | J. exhausted |

1. The _____ movie we watched last night was so odd we left the theater in stunned silence.

2. Ted had _____ about crossing the swinging bridge up over the ravine, since he had been planning this for a long time.

3. The store displayed _____ books that were once read during the 1900s next to vintage hippie clothing.

4. After spending all day cleaning my room and studying for my final exams, I was totally _____.

5. My daughter is quick to complain about what she considers to be a _____ allowance.

6. The weeds growing in my yard were so _____ that they were killing my grass.

7. Nicole had the _____ she could paint her room by herself, but it was not a good idea.

8. He _____ both of my hands in joy as the Jaguars scored a touchdown.

9. After the tough _____, we were offered a raise in pay.

10. When Christian is very hungry, he _____ his food.

# Vocabulary Quiz Answer Key: Prologue and Chapters 1-4

1. The bizarre movie we watched last night was so odd we left the theater in stunned silence.

2. Ted had anticipation about crossing the swinging bridge up over the ravine, since he had been planning this for a long time.

3. The store displayed antique books that were once read during the 1900s next to vintage hippie clothing.

4. After spending all day cleaning my room and studying for my final exams, I was totally exhausted.

5. My daughter is quick to complain about what she considers to be a meager allowance.

6. The weeds growing in my yard were so aggressive that they were killing my grass.

7. Nicole had the notion she would paint her room by herself, but it was not a good idea.

8. He grasps both of my hands in joy, joining us both together as the Jaguars scored a touchdown.

9. After the tough negotiations, we were offered a raise in pay.

10. When Christian is very hungry, he devours his food.

Answer Key:

1. C
2. F
3. B
4. J
5. D

6. G
7. A
8. E
9. H
10. I

Name:_____ Date:_____

## Questions: Prologue and Chapters 1-4

1. What were the two outcomes of the dreams Junior was having?

_____
_____
_____
_____

2. At what age did the family friend tell Junior's mother to give him the special gift for his birthday?

_____
_____
_____
_____

3. Where did Ian attend school? What were the other boys like there?

_____
_____
_____
_____

4. Why did Ian enjoy the antique bookstore?

_____
_____
_____
_____

5. What did Ian's parents give him for his seventeenth birthday?

_____
_____
_____
_____

6. Where did Ian go to look for his parents? Why?

7. When Ian woke up in the taxi, where did he think he was going? Where was he really going?

8. What upset Ian so much at his surprise birthday party? Why?

9. What story did Kayla tell about her and Ian? Why did she tell it?

10. Do you think it's possible for someone to forget a year of their life? What would you do if something like this happened to you? What would you do?

# Answer Key: Prologue and Chapters 1-4 Questions

1. What were the two outcomes of the dreams Junior was having? Total mass destruction and the aftermath of war.

2. At what age did the family friend tell Junior's mother to give him the special gift for his birthday? 18 years old.

3. Where did Ian attend school? What were the other boys like there? Ian attends a public high school in Brooklyn that is filled with over aggressive, muscular guys his age with less than average IQs.

4. Why did Ian enjoy the antique bookstore? It was a place where he could be himself. With no worries about what other kids thought of him while he was at the bookstore, he enjoyed the feeling he got while lost for hours on end in the stories he would read there.

5. What did Ian's parents give him for his seventeenth birthday? An antique timepiece he's been eyeing at the bookstore.

6. Where did Ian go to look for his parents? Why? Ian went to Belvedere Castle in Central Park to look for his parents because his mother took him there many times when he was younger.

7. When Ian woke up in the taxi, where did he think he was going? Where was he really going? When Ian woke up in the taxi, he thought he was headed to Central Park to look for his parents on his seventeenth birthday, but he was actually headed back to Brooklyn to his surprise eighteenth birthday party.

8. What upset Ian so much at his surprise birthday party? Why? The cake said "happy 18th birthday" and Ian thought it was his seventeenth birthday.

9. What story did Kayla tell about her and Ian? Why did she tell it? Kayla told the story about a time she and Ian stayed up to watch a scary movie and were scared for some time after. She told it to ease tensions due to Ian's strange expression on his face.

10. Do you think it's possible for someone to forget a year of their life? What would you do if something like this happened to you? **Student responses will vary due to personal thoughts and experiences.**

## Themes: friendship, dreams, fears, bullying

Throughout this novel, there are several themes that can be explored with students in many ways. These activities should be assigned and completed throughout the novel study, not in just one or two weeks. Here are the themes with a few suggestions on how to use the activities in the classroom either whole class, small group, or individually.

## Suggested Activities:

1. Write and/or tell about a friendship you have had for several years. Tell how you met, why you are friends, and if you think you would remain friends if one of you moved far away. Would you stay in touch and visit each other?

2. Write or tell about a fear you have. Tell what the fear is and how it affects you or others. How can you overcome your fear? Do you think others have the same fear?

3. Write or tell about some dreams that you have had that you remember. Did they seem real? Did they come true? Tell if they relate to anything or anyone you know. Tell if you have had nightmares, either once or reoccurring, and what they may have been about and if you did anything about them.

4. Write about a time that maybe you or someone you know have been bullied. Without using actual names, describe what happened and what was done about the situation. What would you do if you or someone you know were bullied? Would you report it if you saw someone else being bullied? Discuss the bullying policy at your school.

## Extended Activities:

1. Find Brooklyn and New York City on a map. Find out how many miles apart they are. Determine how long it should take Ian to get from his apartment in Brooklyn to New York by taxi.
2. Research Belvedere Castle. Find out when it was built, who built it, and what is meant by a "Victorian folly". Discover if the author was correct with his dates of the castle being built, closed and reopened to the public. Draw Belvedere Castle including the mock Gothic tower.
3. Research the pocket watch. Find out who invented it and when. Check back in the novel to see if the author was correct about it. Draw a pocket watch. Do you think people would want to use a pocket watch today? Why or why not?
4. Write About It: Do you believe objects such as a pocket watch could be magic or hold special powers? Why or why not? Would you want an object with special powers? Which powers? What would you do with special powers?

Belvedere Castle

Novel Study by Patricia Carpenter

Name:_____  Date:_____

# Test: Prologue and Chapters 1-4

1. What is the name of the place Ian knew about to go look for his parents after they left the apartment without telling him? Why?

_____
_____
_____
_____

2. What did "Jax" tell Ian about the watch? List at least two.

_____
_____
_____
_____

3. Why was Junior disturbed by his dreams? What were the dreams?

_____
_____
_____
_____

4. What was Junior going to do about his dreams? What's his plan?

_____
_____
_____
_____

5. Why didn't Ian like to ride in a taxi?

_____
_____
_____
_____

6. What happened to Ian during his taxi ride?

_____
_____
_____

7. When Ian returned home to his apartment, he was surprised in several ways. Tell at least 3 ways Ian was surprised.

_____
_____
_____

8. Who is Alexis? What did she give to Kayla and why?

_____
_____
_____

9. Why was Kayla going to attend her senior year of high school without her best friend Ian?

_____
_____
_____

10. What does Ian's father tell him to do? Does he do as his father asked?

_____
_____
_____

Novel Study by Patricia Carpenter

# Test Answers Prologue and Chapters 1-4

1. What is the name of the place Ian knew of to go look for his parents after they left the apartment without telling him? Why? He went to Belvedere Castle in Central Park because his mom took him there when he was young.

2. What did "Jax" tell Ian about the watch? List at least two. The watch can store memories, it can change history, it has been in his family for generations, it has powers, it was invented by Peter Hele, Ian accessed it by accident, Ian's dreams are actual moments in time.

3. Why was Junior disturbed by his dreams? What were the dreams? Junior's dreams were really nightmares of the future of total mass destruction of the Earth or the aftermath of war. He knew these could be future memories.

4. What was Junior going to do about his dreams? What's his plan? Junior remembered stories his mother told him of a family friend, Ian. Junior has to find Ian to help Junior from being deleted from history.

5. Why didn't Ian like to ride in a taxi? Horrible smell, & the way taxi drivers drove with eyes closed and changing lanes without looking.

6. What happened to Ian during his taxi ride? He was on his way to Belvedere Castle in the morning and suddenly it was dark outside and he was headed back to Brooklyn.

7. When Ian returned home to his apartment, he was surprised in several ways. Tell at least three ways Ian was surprised. The surprise party, getting a gift from Kayla, the cake saying 'happy 18th birthday'.

8. Who is Alexis? What did she give to Kayla and why? Alexis and Kayla had met before, but Kayla didn't remember it. Alexis wanted Kayla to give Ian a birthday gift for her since she would not be able to return next year to give it to him herself.

9. Why was Kayla going to attend her senior year of high school without her best friend Ian? For the first time since they had met and had become friends, Kayla and Ian were going to attend separate schools since Ian was going to a special school.

10. What does Ian's father tell him to do? Does he do as his father asked? Ian's father told him to go lie down and get some rest which he did, falling asleep quickly.

# Summaries: Chapters 5-10

**Chapter 5:** After quickly falling asleep, Ian has a series of four dreams. One is where he wakes up in a king's bed, the next he's in an old fashioned classroom, then he's on a park bench where he meets "Jax" who tells him a little bit about the time keeper, and finally he's at a party in a penthouse. He is awakened in his own bed by a knock at his bedroom door. It's Kayla.

**Chapter 6:** Kayla has Ian open the birthday gift she gave him, but it's from Alexis yet Ian is unaware of this fact. It is a silver ring. Ian then tells Kayla about his four dreams and she repeats them back to him making the mistake of calling the watch the time keeper which leads Ian to believe Kayla knows more than she is saying.

**Chapter 7:** Ian puts on the time keeper watch and the ring Kayla had given him. Once the two are together on his wrist and finger, a flood of memories rush through him, only they are going backwards. At the same time, Kayla experiences the rush of wind and falling through nothingness, and then she loses consciousness. She awakens with Alexis who explains some things to Kayla. Ian goes to Kayla's apartment for help, but she doesn't live there and never has according to the people who answer the door. Ian needs help, so he decides to go back to Central Park to try to find Jax.

**Chapter 8:** Ian thinks it's better to take the subway into Central Park this time. On the subway he has time to wonder about things like, why is it his seventeenth birthday again, what happened to Kayla, and why doesn't she live in her apartment? Ian notices a little girl on the train that holds his attention for some reason and then his watch and ring vibrate. But luckily nothing happens this time. Once off the subway train, Ian continues to Central Park to search for Jax.

**Chapter 9:** Fortunately, Ian does meet Jax in the park. Ian tells Jax about Kayla not living in her apartment. Jax is concerned about Ian's parents, but Ian assures him they are fine. Ian wants Jax to tell him more about the watch and its powers, but Jax says he has to tell Ian about the history of the time keeper first.

**Chapter 10:** Jax tells Ian that Peter Hele invented the pocket watch. Jax explained that Peter not only invented a way to tell time but also a way to store moments in time to be revisited later. These moments could be changed, but it would or could also change future events in history, so it had to be done carefully, if at all. Only Peter Hele and his descendants could store and later access these moments in time. Jax told Ian how the watch was lost for generations until his parents found it and bought it for him for his eighteenth birthday. Ian and Jax then decide to return to Ian's apartment to discuss all of this with Ian's parents.

## Vocabulary: Chapters 5-10

Write these words on the board and have the students define each word, use in a sentence, find synonyms, locate in the novel, and discuss whole class or small group:

1. exquisite
2. resemble
3. antiquated
4. extreme
5. inquisitive
6. retrieve
7. boasting
8. retort
9. recognize
10. intuition
11. challenging
12. preoccupation
13. suspicions
14. compelled
15. previously

History Series – Time Keeper

Name:_____ Date:_____

# Chapters 5-10 Vocabulary Word Search

```
N U D U H L U L R K Y Y U U B F W D Q T R L Q O
W W W F J H V O E T A K I T F D N X A I Z X E J
F C J Z M D Z B T T W I R A K S M V G I P V T I
Z M Q E C M X B O G B P F I F T Q J S G S F L E
T T E S E I J P R E O C C U P A T I O N X U F V
O K O C V C Z J T L A X N D H W Y L N Q V D H I
F C H A L L E N G I N G L U S E L Z W X D Q C T
N J Y R K O P N S F W L K Z R N K U G N B Q P I
D I Y E D M E E L P D H A E M G W R I V C U G S
E S L B D L Z W N Z B V T K S V Z I T B H G G I
T F N M K P I Q W U U R V U V A O N U R N U N U
A L U Y I Z N G I P I N S N G J J S Y I M M O Q
U A H V Q T G B E E T P A R Z M Y K T V E N I N
Q M T L N I O Z V W I T Z Z D Q R S E S M V T I
I P V Q D T C E W C E P I F Z Q A N X T E D I S
T A J V V Q E C I R U D D H V O Y A Q G R P U S
N M R P A V R O B E Q Y E O B Y K N U Q T N T P
A F Z V V A N I T S S D S L Y D K M I U X W N Q
D I J K T S T I C E C O N U L C F L S A E V I L
P J N G V G O P B M F E E S V E I M I F Y E Y D
Z P C F D Q O Q S B J M I W W I P J T R R M K X
H Z T I U Y C O K L X A S H J L P M E A C M C I
Q I P G S M M A B E N C O M W L O U O L D W B X
C V X G P R E V I O U S L Y L H Q M Y C M A X N
```

previously        n challenging      extreme
retort            intuition          antiquated
compelled         recognize          resemble
suspicions        boasting           exquisite
preoccupatio      inquisitive        retrieve

Novel Study by Patricia Carpenter

# Answer Key: Chapters 5-10 Vocabulary Word Search

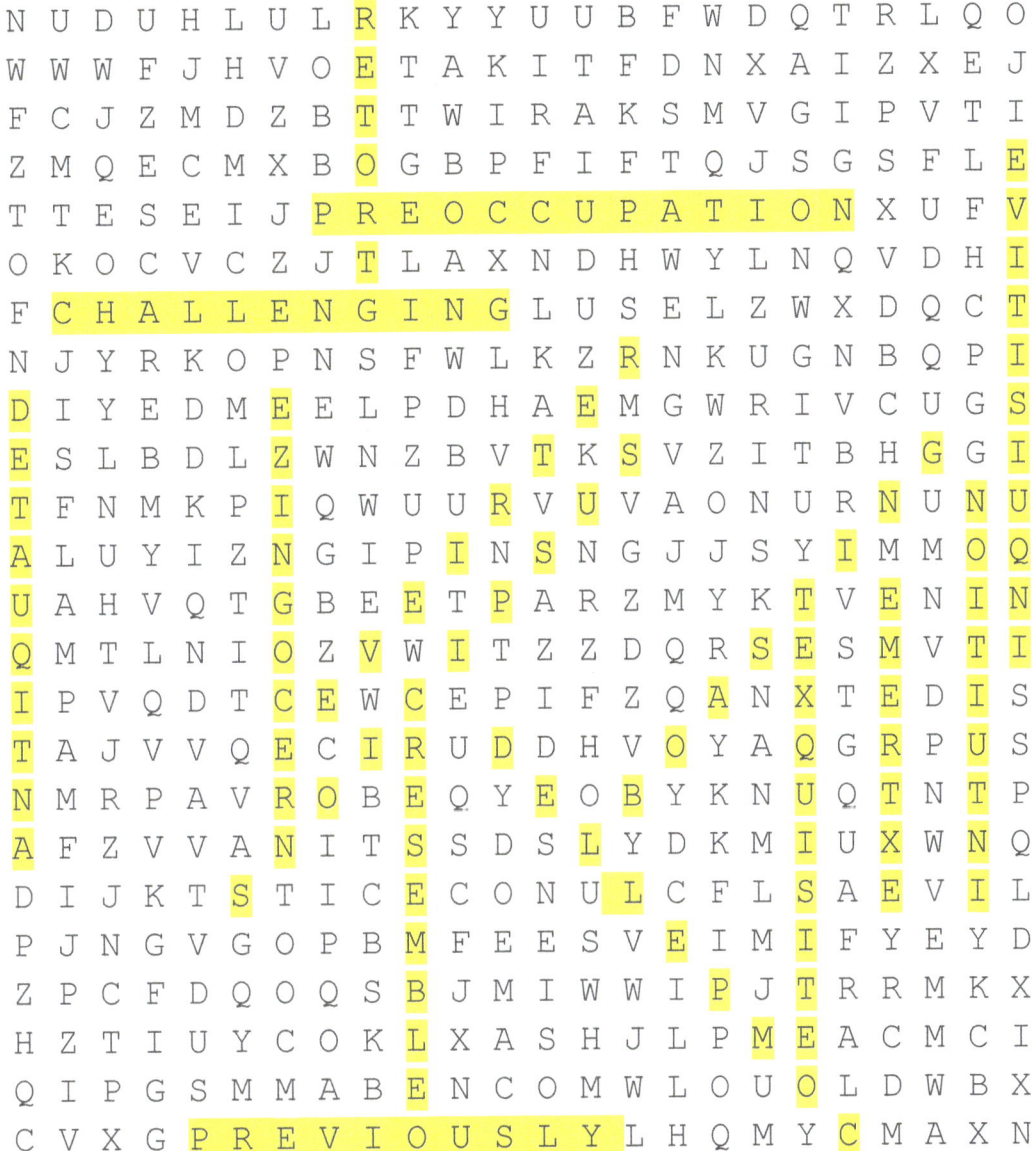

previously        challenging       extreme
retort            intuition         antiquated
compelled         recognize         resemble
suspicions        boasting          exquisite
preoccupation     inquisitive       retrieve

History Series – Time Keeper

Name:_____  Date:_____

## Chapter 5 Activity

Chapter 5 is about the four dreams Ian experiences. The dreams are very descriptive and use a lot of imagery. Using the novel, complete the following activity for Chapter 5.

1. Name the pieces of furniture, architecture, and objects in the bedroom in the first dream. Use the complete description of each. Use all of the adjectives to describe each item.

    Example: "small, lovely lavender flowers..." not just "flowers".

_____
_____
_____
_____
_____
_____

2. Ian found the classroom in his second dream to be very different from his classroom at his school today. List at least 5 things that are unique to the classroom in Ian's dream.

    1. _____
    2. _____
    3. _____
    4. _____
    5. _____

3. What was the man, "Jax", wearing when Ian met him in the park?

___

4. Describe the setting of Ian's fourth and final dream.

___

# Chapter 5 Activity Answer Key

1. Name the pieces of furniture, architecture, and objects in the bedroom in the first dream. Use the complete description of each. Use all of the adjectives to describe each item.

   Example: "small, lovely lavender flowers..." not just "flowers".

gray concrete walls covered in oversized paintings; enormous, elegant four post bed; two hand crafted, wood, wingback chairs; exquisite handmade rug; arches of the cathedral ceilings are painted with angels and biblical themes; bright red wallpaper, gold paint trim of the six foot tall fireplace; crystal candle chandelier

2. Ian found the classroom in his second dream to be very different from his classroom at his school today. List at least 5 things that are unique to the classroom in Ian's dream.

   1. uncomfortable hardwood student desks for two students each
   2. wood burning furnace with a metal pipe going out of the ceiling on a wood floor
   3. a freestanding wooden globe
   4. two oil lamps
   5. an old, interesting looking piano

3. What was the man, "Jax", wearing when Ian met him in the park? The strange man is dressed in a tracksuit, running shoes, and red headphones that hang around his neck.

4. Describe the setting of Ian's fourth and final dream. The room he is in is on the top floor penthouse of a high-rise in Manhattan. From the floor-to-ceiling windows, Ian can make out Belvedere Castle. The room is massive, wall to wall windows giving a panoramic view. Not only can Ian see Belvedere Castle in Central Park, but as he turns around he can see the entire city of New York City.

History Series – Time Keeper

Name:_____  Date:_____

# Test: Chapters 5-10

1. List the 4 places of Ian's dream memories.
_____
_____
_____
_____

2. What two pieces of jewelry did Ian wear and what happened when he wore them together?
_____
_____
_____
_____

3. What advice did Kayla give to Ian about his dreams?
_____
_____
_____
_____

4. Why did Ian begin to think Kayla knew more about what was happening to him than she was telling?
_____
_____
_____
_____

5. Who is "Jax"? Describe him. Why is he important to the story?

6. Who is with Kayla when she first regains consciousness? What do we already know about this character?

7. How did the term "pocket watch" originate?

8. How did the time keeper get lost and why is this important?

9. Who was the man that was murdered for his wrist watch? Why was his important?

_____
_____
_____
_____
_____
_____

10. Where were Jax and Ian headed at the end of Chapter 10? Why?

_____
_____
_____
_____
_____
_____

Novel Study by Patricia Carpenter

# Test Answer Key Chapters 5-10

1. List the 4 places of Ian's dream memories. <u>Bedroom fit for a king, an old fashioned classroom, a park bench in central park, a party in a penthouse.</u>

2. What two pieces of jewelry did Ian wear and what happened when he wore them together? <u>The watch and the ring from Kayla, they vibrate when worn together and some memories came flooding into Ian's head fast and backwards, Kayla disappeared.</u>

3. What advice did Kayla give to Ian about his dreams? <u>She told him he should ask his parents about what was happening to him.</u>

4. Why did Ian begin to think Kayla knew more about what was happening to him than she was telling? <u>When Kayla was telling Ian's dreams back to him, she called the watch the time keeper which Ian had not told her. So he started to think she knew more than she was saying. Plus she had never given him a gift before and he felt the ring vibrate.</u>

5. Who is "Jax"? Describe him. Why is he important to the story? <u>"Jax" is wearing a tracksuit and red headphones. He is a teacher at a special school who has met Ian before even though Ian doesn't remember. He told Ian the history of the watch, how it's been in his family for generations, and about its powers.</u>

6. Who is with Kayla when she first regains consciousness? What do we already know about this person? <u>When Kayla wakes up, Alexis is there with her. Alexis is the person who met Kayla in the stairwell of the apartment building and gave her a gift for Ian which turned out to be a silver ring.</u>

7. How did the term "pocket watch" originate? During the 17th century a chain was added to it, which was called a fob. The fob then made it possible for men to be able to start wearing watches in their pockets without the worry of losing them. You see, one end of the chain was attached to the watch while the other end had a clasp, which they could attach to their jacket allowing the actual watch to be carried in their pockets. Hence the familiar term, 'Pocket Watch', which you hear today

8. How did the time keeper get lost and why is this important? Sebastian and Greyson were fighting one night behind a pub and the time keeper was lost in the fight, and now Sebastian can no longer go back and fix his relationship with Greyson nor can her pass it down to his descendants

9. Who was the man that was murdered for his wrist watch? Why was this important? A man found murdered over his wrist watch, the murderer stated someone had hired him to kill this man and steal his watch. Then the Believers unraveled the truth about the murdered man. He was a descendant of the Hele family bloodline.

10. Where were Jax and Ian headed at the end of Chapter 10? Why? They will hail a cab to take them to Ian's home where his questions can all be answered in detail, first priority is for Ian's arrival home and to talk to his parents, Ian is the one who is missing now, instead of them, on his first seventeenth birthday

Name:_____  Date:_____

# Chapters 5-10 Vocabulary Quiz

Directions: Put the letter of the word that matches the definition in the blank.

1. lovely, beautiful, delicate
2. old fashioned, outdated
3. get or bring something back
4. say something back sharply
5. look or seem like something else
6. instinct, good sense
7. identify someone or something from before
8. brag, overstate
9. curious, inquiring
10. large amount, severe, bad
11. before, formally, earlier
12. force, pressure someone, urge
13. feeling, idea, possibility
14. concentrate, thinking, day dreaming
15. testing one's abilities; demanding

A. recognize
B. retort
C. antiquated
D. challenging
E. compelled
F. preoccupation
G. inquisitive
H. previously
I. suspicions
J. intuition
K. resemble
L. bragging
M. extreme
N. exquisite
O. retrieve

History Series – Time Keeper

# Chapters 5-10 Vocabulary Quiz Answers

1. lovely, beautiful, delicate — N — A. recognize
2. old fashioned, outdated — C — B. retort
3. get or bring something back — O — C. antiquated
4. say something back sharply — B — D. challenging
5. look or seem like something else — K — E. compelled
6. instinct, good sense — J — F. preoccupation
7. identify someone or something from before — A — G. inquisitive
8. brag, overstate — L — H. previously
9. curious, inquiring — G — I. suspicions
10. large amount, severe, bad — M — J. intuition
11. before, formally, earlier — H — K. resemble
12. force, pressure someone, urge — E — L. bragging
13. feeling, idea, possibility — I — M. extreme
14. concentrate, thinking, day dreaming — F — N. exquisite
15. testing one's abilities; demanding — D — O. retrieve

# Summaries: Chapters 11-16 and Epilogue

**Chapter 11:** Jax tells Ian more about the time keeper and how to store a memory one must focus on one particular object so the memory can be accessed in the future. This leads Ian to wonder about the "red" objects in each one of the memory dreams he was shown.

**Chapter 12:** Jax explains the relationship between the Helen and Zimmerman bloodlines. They always become friends in the beginning, best friends one can say, but in the end, they always become enemies with a fight of some kind or another.

**Chapter 13:** Jax tells Ian about Mason Carpenter who was one of the Believers who wanted the time keeper for himself. He tried to steal it from police evidence, but that didn't work out. Ian tells Jax that Kayla was the one who gave him the ring for his birthday; he thinks she knows more about what's happening that she is telling him, and about the memory wipe that wiped Kayla from history, from everyone except Ian.

**Chapter 14:** Ian and Jax arrive back at Ian's apartment to find his parents there and well. They try to explain how they met in Central Park, how Jax told Ian about the watch's history, and that Ian needs to get to the school with Jax. Alexis fills Kayla in on how her connection with Ian works. Kayla makes contact with Ian through their bond. Alexis gives Kayla some memories to help her.

**Chapter 15:** Kayla wakes up and meets Mason, yet she's not sure who he is. She has a headache and asks to take a bath. Later Mason tries to question her and that's when the memories Alexis gave her help her deal with things. Kayla sends another message to Ian, "Don't forget me Ian".

**Chapter 16:** While sleeping, Ian begins to have more visions, or dream memories, but he knows they are not from Kayla but from someone he has never met. He is in a white room, with a little boy and girl he does not recognize. Several bizarre things happen before Ian finally meets the one in control, Junior, who as it turns out is Kayla's son from the future. Because she wiped herself from history, Junior is now fading from Ian's mind. Then, through their bond, Kayla reaches out to Ian and asks that he not forget her.

**Epilogue:** Junior fades away, the Council is aware history has changed; they are seeking help from Alexis. They search their birth and death records for "Kayla Alexis" to no avail, and they realize Alexis erased herself from history, and they have no way to go back and change anything. Ian also is searching for a way back in history to find Alexis. So who will find her first?

## Vocabulary: Chapters 11-16 and Epilogue

Write these words on the board and have the students define each word, use in a sentence, find synonyms, locate in the novel, and discuss whole class or small group:

| | | |
|---|---|---|
| advantage | concept | achievable |
| generations | alternative | speculating |
| ancestors | disastrous | terminates |
| possessed | sensational | stern |
| privileges | anticipate | confident |

History Series – Time Keeper

Name:_____  Date:_____

# Chapters 11-16 & Epilogue Vocabulary Crossword

Directions: Choose the word that matches the clue and write it in the puzzle.

- 44 -

Novel Study by Patricia Carpenter

Directions: Choose the word that matches the clue and write it in the puzzle.

## Down

| 1 | A general idea derived from specific instances |
|---|---|
| 2 | Events having unfortunate or dire outcomes, bringing ruin |
| 3 | Assurance, self reliance, trustful |
| 4 | Having a more favorable position |
| 5 | To succeed, successful, obstainable |
| 6 | Causing intense interest, curiosity, or emotion |

## Across

| 4 | Regarding something that can probably or likely, to expect |
|---|---|
| 6 | To believe on uncertain or tentative grounds, curious or doubtful |
| 7 | Strict demeanor |
| 8 | One from a number of things that can be chosen |

## Word Bank:

confident   disastrous   sensational   anticipate
speculating   concept   alternative
advantage   achievable   stern

## Chapters 11-16 & Epilogue Vocabulary Crossword

Answer Key

Down

| 1 | Concept |
| 2 | Disastrous |
| 3 | Confident |
| 4 | Advantage |
| 5 | Acheivable |
| 6 | Sensational |

Across

| 4 | Anticipate |
| 6 | Speculation |
| 7 | Stern |
| 8 | Alternative |

Novel Study by Patricia Carpenter

Name:_____ Date:_____

# Chapters 11-16 & Epilogue Vocabulary Quiz

Directions: Circle the word that matches the meaning of the sentence or definition.

1. What word means unfortunate or dire outcomes?

    A. concept B. alternative

    C. disastrous D. sensational

2. The person in the front row had a more favorable seat that the man in the back.

    A. confident B. advantage

    C. stern D. speculating

3. The people were uncertain and doubtful of the outcome of the race.

    A. confident B. concept

    C. stern D. speculating

4. The Big Bang Theory is a general idea derived from specific instances.

    A. alternative B. disastrous

    C. concept D. sensational

5. The great ball player had many colleges to choose from to attend.

    A. disastrous B. alternatives

    C. concept D. advantage

6. The preacher had a very strict demeanor.

　　A. confident B. stern

　　C. speculating D. achievable

7. What word means probably or likely or to expect?

　　A. achievable B. anticipate

　　C. speculating D. stern

8. What word means causing intense interest, curiosity, or emotion?

　　A. disastrous B. concept

　　C. sensational D. speculating

9. The scholarly student knew he could succeed and obtain his goal.

　　A. achievable B. anticipate

　　C. concept D. sensational

10. The good looking young man was full of assurance and self-reliance, so he knew the girl would go on a date with him.

　　A. disastrous B. stern

　　C. concept D. confident

Novel Study by Patricia Carpenter

# Chapters 11-16 & Epilogue Vocabulary Quiz

# Answer Key

1. C
2. B
3. D
4. C
5. B
6. B
7. B
8. C
9. A
10. D

History Series – Time Keeper

Name:_____  Date:_____

# Chapters 11-16 & Epilogue Questions

1. What objects were "red" in Ian's dream memories? Why is this important?

_____
_____
_____
_____

2. Why did the training at the school stop on how to use the watch?

_____
_____
_____
_____

3. What happened to Sebastian and Grayson to end their friendship? Why couldn't Sebastian fix it?

_____
_____
_____
_____

4. Who is Mason Carpenter and how did he gain possession of the watch?

_____
_____
_____
_____

5. What did the thief do with the watch?

_____
_____
_____

6. When Ian returned home, what had changed about Ian's parents this time, since there had been a change in history?

_____
_____
_____
_____

7. What is the special bond between Ian and Kayla?

_____
_____
_____
_____

8. Why did Alexis have to put Kayla into a deep sleep?

9. What were the two kinds of memories Alexis gave to Kayla, and what are they used for?

10. Who does Ian find out has been controlling his dream memories? How is this person connected to another character in the novel?

# Chapters 11-16 & Epilogue Questions

Answers

1. What objects were "red" in Ian's dream memories? Why is this important? <u>The first memory was a room in which one wall was covered with red wallpaper, the second memory was of an old school classroom and at the head of the room was the teachers' desk which had a single red apple on top of it, the red apple wasn't out of place, it's just that this memory was in black and white except for the apple, the third one the object was the red headphones you are wearing now around your neck right now, the last memory is not of a time happening yet, but a man at a party is wearing a tuxedo with a red bow tie. This is a way to label memories to be accessed later.</u>

2. Why did the training stop at the school on how to use the watch? <u>Without the time keeper, since it had been lost for so many years, no Hele bloodline would have been in control of the time keeper, so no need to train others on how to use the time keeper.</u>

3. What happened to Sebastian and Grayson to end their friendship? Why couldn't Sebastian fix it? <u>They had a big fight, and after their last fight, with Sebastian's inability to find the time keeper and store the horrible fight between them in the time keeper, with the time keeper being lost, he would never be able to go back and change the outcome of that moment in time. From that point on, their bloodlines' destinies have been in a cycle of repeating the same events, becoming friends and then enemies.</u>

4. Who is Mason Carpenter and how did he gain possession of the watch? The Believers, found out one of our own, Mason Carpenter, was a descendant of Grayson, he started looking for the time keeper. He paid off a police officer to retrieve the watch from police evidence to give to him. The police officer does what he is paid to do, and once Mason has possession of the time keeper, he heads home. After Mason is safe and secure at home, he reaches into his pocket to retrieve the watch and then realizes his pocket is empty. He feels that all the trouble he has gone through to get the time keeper was for nothing. The time keeper is missing again, and Mason cannot think of how he lost such a small object on his way home. He only had possession of the watch for a short time. Mason begins to recall every place he passed on his way home. He thinks of every person's face he crossed paths with on his way home, and then he remembers bumping into a young man. Mason did not think that the innocent looking young man could have been anything more than just a classic case of not watching where he was going. That was until he realized the watch had gone missing upon his arrival home.

5. What did the thief do with the watch?
The thief needed to get rid of the watch as soon as possible, his friend worked at an old book store, he set up a meeting with the owner and sold the watch to him. The owner gave a great deal for the watch.

6. When Ian returned home, what had changed about Ian's parents this time, since there had been a change in history? When Ian came out of his room on his seventeenth birthday, his parents had been kidnapped, this time they both we at home, safe.

7. What is the special bond between Ian and Kayla?
Kayla has to try to reach out to Ian. "Ian! Can you hear me? It's me, Kayla," she speaks with her mind. "Can you hear me?" he can hear the sound of HER voice in his mind. Their lives were destined to cross paths from the time they were born.

8. Why did Alexis have to put Kayla into a deep sleep?
Kayla is in the deep sleep Alexis put her in to receive the memories she needed.

9. What are the two types of memories Alexis gives to Kayla and what are they used for?
Some of these memories will be real, while others will be fake. The fake ones are only there to help you survive until we figure out how to bring you back safely. You will not understand them at first, but you will when you wake up. I am asking you to put a lot more trust in me, but I will never lie to you or put you in danger. You will be able to tell which ones are for you and which ones are for your survival.

10. Who does Ian find out has been controlling his dream memories? How is this person connected to another character in the novel?
You may call me Junior, "Kayla. Her name is Kayla," Ian answers. "Mom," whispers Junior. So now we can assume Kayla is Junior's mother.

History Series – Time Keeper

# ACT IT OUT

**Teachers:** Do this activity as it fits your classroom and your students.

In small groups or whole class, each student acts out one of the characters: Ian, Kayla, Jax, Junior, Ian's mom, Ian's dad or Alexis. They chose a character, or the teacher assigns each student a character, and then they answer questions from the other students as that character. Example: If a student were to be "Jax", someone might ask them what they had around their neck when they met Ian in the park. The answer would be: red headphones. Continue with the activity as time permits.

# Saving History Series: Time Keeper Bingo Card Activity

Teachers: Make copies of the bingo card on the following page. Each student should have their own card. Write all of the vocabulary words from the book on the board and let the students chose any of those words and print them in the squares of the bingo card, one word per square.

Play the Bingo game any way you wish, 5 in a row, diagonal, X, blackout, or any other way. Read a definition of a vocabulary word and have the students mark their card if they have that word.

| | | |
|---|---|---|
| notion | antiquated | previously |
| anticipation | extreme | intuition |
| antique | inquisitive | recognize |
| aggressive | retrieve | confident |
| bizarre | boasting | speculating |
| negotiations | retort | advantage |
| meager | anticipate | sensational |
| devours | challenging | disastrous |
| grasps | preoccupation | concept |
| exhausted | suspicions | achievable |
| exquisite | compelled | alternative |
| resemble | | stern |

Name:_____    Date:_____

# Saving History Series: Time Keeper Bingo Card

| B | I | N | G | O |
|---|---|---|---|---|
|   |   |   |   |   |
|   |   |   |   |   |
|   |   | **Free Space** |   |   |
|   |   |   |   |   |
|   |   |   |   |   |

# Essay Contest

**Teachers:** Write these directions for the essay contest on the board.

Write a 250 word essay about book 1 of the "Saving History Series: Time Keeper." You should put yourself in Ian's place and decide what you should do about Kayla. Should you continue to try to find her and return her to your timeline, even if it means some things will unexpectedly change for you? How far are you willing to go to find your friend, even if it puts you or your family in danger? What do you think about the connection between Kayla and Junior? What will happen to Junior if Kayla remains "lost"? What exciting things would you like to have happen to Ian and Kayla in Book Two, 'School Bound?'

**Teachers: Please submit the top five essays to contest@starnesbooksllc.com. The winner will receive a personalized, autographed copy of the novel from the author.**